Dedicated to all the strange kids who love monsters,
wherever you may be.

Lil' LIBROS
www.LilLibros.com

Kid del Toro
Published by Little Libros, LLC
Text © 2021 Chogrin
Art © 2021 Pakoto
Translation © 2021 Little Libros, LLC
Library of Congress Control Number 2021935759
Printed in China
First Edition—2021
26 25 24 23 22 21   5 4 3 2 1
ISBN 978-1-947971-68-4

This is an independently authored and published account of a childhood experience of Guillermo del Toro
as heard through public interviews, and no affiliation with or endorsement by Mr. del Toro is claimed or implied.

KID DEL TORO

WRITTEN BY
CHOGRIN

ART BY
PAKOTO

Lil' LIBROS

Guillermo was a special kid. He liked to stay
at home with his books. He read about insects,
the paranormal, but especially
about MONSTERS!

Guillermo era un niño especial.
Lo que más le gustaba era quedarse
en casa con sus libros. Le gustaba leer sobre
insectos y cosas paranormales, pero sobre todo
le gustaba leer sobre ¡MONSTRUOS!

Guillermo loved monsters so much
that he often dressed up as one.
FRANKENSTEIN's monster
was his favorite.

Guillermo amaba tanto a los monstruos
que a menudo se vestía como uno.
Su favorito era el monstruo
de **FRANKENSTEIN**.

What he didn't like
was when Abuela would
send him to bed.
"Those books will give you
nightmares!" she'd say.

Lo que no le gustaba era
cuando Abuela lo mandaba
a dormir. «¡Esos libros
te darán pesadillas!»,
le decía ella.

In his room, Guillermo was restless. All he could think about were his monster books. No problem, he thought. He would sneak out as usual to get them.

En su cuarto, Guillermo estaba
inquieto. Solo podía pensar
en sus libros de monstruos.
No hay problema, pensó.
Se escabulliría como siempre
para conseguirlos.

But when Guillermo was about to get out of bed, he saw something.... It came from behind the sofa. It was a...

Pero cuando Guillermo
estaba a punto de bajarse
de su cama, vio algo...
Estaba detrás del sofá.
Era un...

MONSTER!
It had horns, red eyes,
and it was coming
to eat him!

¡MONSTRUO!

Tenía cuernos, ojos rojos, ¡y se lo iba a comer!

Guillermo was so scared that he screamed!
Poor Guillermo.

¡Guillermo estaba tan asustado que gritó!
Pobre Guillermo.

Suddenly, a noise stirred in the house.
Something that scared him
even more than monsters. It was...

De repente, se oyó un ruido en la casa.
Algo que lo asustaba aún más
que los monstruos. Era...

Abuela! And she was angry.

¡Abuela! Y estaba enojada.

"I told you those books would give
you nightmares," said Abuela. "Go back
to sleep or I'll throw those books away!"

«Te dije que esos libros
te darían pesadillas», dijo Abuela.
«¡Vete a dormir o botaré esos libros!»

The following night Guillermo was determined
to face the monster so he could read
his books in peace.

La noche siguiente, Guillermo estaba
decidido a enfrentarse al monstruo
para poder leer sus libros en paz.

But when the monster appeared again,
something had changed. Its eyes were no longer red.
It even seemed friendly....

Pero cuando el monstruo apareció de nuevo,
algo había cambiado. Sus ojos ya no eran rojos.
De hecho, parecía amigable...

So friendly, in fact, that it shook
Guillermo's hand. That night Guillermo made
a promise to the monster. That if it wouldn't
scare him at night, he would be
its friend forever.

Tan amigable que le dio
la mano a Guillermo. Esa noche,
Guillermo le hizo al monstruo
una promesa. Le prometió que
si no lo asustaba de noche,
sería su amigo para siempre.

And from that night on, they would do everything together. From baking cookies...

Y a partir de esa noche, harían todo juntos. Horneando galletas...

...and making movies...

...y filmando películas...

...to tucking Guillermo into bed.

...y hasta arropando a Guillermo
en su cama.

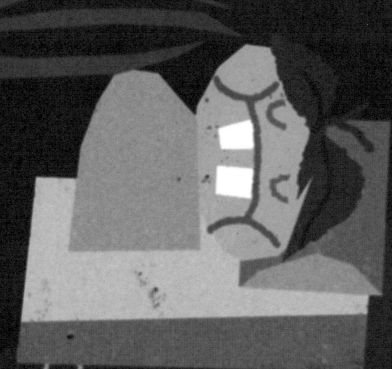

Even Abuela noticed
something in Guillermo
had changed.

Incluso Abuela
notó que algo había
cambiado en Guillermo.

Now Guillermo didn't just read
about monsters, they were also
his friends.

Ahora Guillermo no solo leía
sobre monstruos, también eran
sus amigos.

AUTHOR

Chogrin is an artist and storyteller from Guayaquil, Ecuador. His imagination is fueled by his childhood, science, folklore, and his family and friends. For the last decade he has worked in the animation industry for companies like Cartoon Network and Disney. His artwork has been featured in multiple art galleries and publications around the world. He's currently designing vinyl toys like "Guru del Toro," as well as writing, drawing, and directing many projects from his art laboratory in Burbank, CA.

ILLUSTRATOR

Born in Albacete, Spain, **Pakoto** is an illustrator working in the world of animation. He has done visual development and character design for studios like Reel Fx, Screen Novelties, and Netflix. His artwork has also been featured in numerous galleries around the world, including Gallery 1988, Gallery Nucleus, and Bottleneck Gallery.

Kid del Toro is inspired by the many childhood recollections
and televised interviews given by the Oscar-winning Mexican filmmaker,
Guillermo del Toro. His fascination with childhood, monsters, and the
paranormal is woven into his numerous films and TV shows,
like *Pan's Labyrinth* and *Trollhunters*. It seems like del Toro's
love of monsters is lifelong, since he never forgets to shine
the spotlight on them on the big screen.

¡Viva Guillermo!